Janice VanCleave's

Play and Find Out

about

The Human Body

Easy Experiments for Young Children

John Wiley & Sons, Inc.

New York • Chichester • Weinheim • Brisbane • Singapore • Toronto

Library of Congress Cataloging-in-Publication Data

VanCleave, Janice Pratt.
    [Play and find out about the human body]
    Janice VanCleave's Play and find out about the human body.
    p.   cm.   — (Play and find out series)
    Includes index.
    Summary: Presents simple experiments answering such questions about the human
body as "Why does my skin pucker up when I take a long bath?" "Why are my bones
hard?" and "How much breath do I have?"
    ISBN 0-471-12934-8 (cloth : alk. paper).—ISBN 0-471-12935-6 (pbk. : alk. paper)
    1. Human physiology—Experiments—Juvenile literature. 2. Body, Human—Juvenile
literature. [1. Human physiology—Experiments. 2. Body, Human—Experiments. 3.
Experiments. 4. Questions and answers.] I. Title. II. Series: VanCleave, Janice Pratt. Play
and find out series.
QP37.V364   1998
612—dc21   97-28716

Dedication

This book is dedicated to a teacher who is endless in her search to make learning fun for her students. She field-tested the experiments in this book and not only provided valuable input, but included pictures of her sweetie-pie students performing the experiments. What a delight it is to work with my colleague and friend, Laura Fields Roberts.

Acknowledgments

I wish to express my appreciation to the following teachers and students, who assisted me in testing the experiments in this book:

St. Matthew's Elementary School (Louisville, Kentucky) students, under the direction of Laura Fields Roberts and her coworker, Sandra Williams Petrey: Tricia Baldwin, Brittany Ballinger, Amanda Boden, Antonio Brown, Stephanie Coy, Joshlyn Cross-Stone, Jovan Dawson, Courtney Duffey, Alexandria Foote, Kaitlin Goodhew, Chelsey Hallett, Jessica Hamilton, Dane Hardy, Taylor Hawkins, Emily Jimmerson, William Long, Amy Love, Saphire Miller, Taylor Mouser, David Presnell, Hannah Rapp, Kristin Shattuck, Beth Spurr, Sarah Thomas, and Orenzio Tobin. A special note of thanks also to the principal of St. Matthew's, Donna Kelly Duncan, for her support of this project in her school.

A special home-schooling family donated time to test and provide valuable input about experiments. The adult learning facilitators of this group are Ron and Anne Skrabanek. Not only did they involve their own children, Sarah, Benjamin, and Rebecca, in this project, but they also shared the materials with the following home schoolers in the Homeschool–Co-op (Waco, Texas), including Greg, Mona, Bethany, and Michael Bond; Ken, Carol, Matthew, Emily, and Sarah Keil; Kent, Debbie, Anna, Kent Jr., Steven, and Andrew Mathias; and John, Diana, Joseph, Abigail, and Samuel Warren.

A thank-you is also expressed to Debbie Karlovetz, a teacher at Owen Elementary (Tyler, Texas). Debbie read the experiments and gave many helpful suggestions.

It was my honor to have a former colleague and friend, Sändra Kilpatrick, field-test some of the experiments with her daughter, Katie Kilpatrick (Fort Smith, Arkansas). Sändra and Katie and everyone listed contributed greatly to making this book more fun.

Contents

A Letter from Janice VanCleave   1

Before You Begin   2

Skin

Ridged   *I Wonder . . . Why Do My Fingertips Have Ridges?*   6

Pleated   *I Wonder . . . Why Are My Elbows Wrinkly?*   10

Puckered   *I Wonder . . . Why Does My Skin Pucker Up When I Take a Long Bath?*   14

Darker   *I Wonder . . . Why Does My Skin Tan?*   18

Keeping Cool   *I Wonder . . . Why Do I Sweat?*   22

Hair

Hairy   *I Wonder . . . Why Do I Have Hair on My Body?*   26

Curly   *I Wonder . . . . Why Is My Hair Curly?*   30

Painless   *I Wonder . . . Why Doesn't My Hair Hurt When It Gets Cut?*   34

Skeleton

Movable   *I Wonder . . . How Does My Back Bend?*   40

Rubbery   *I Wonder . . . Why Are My Bones Hard?*   44

Bendable   *I Wonder . . . Why Do My Arms Bend?*   48

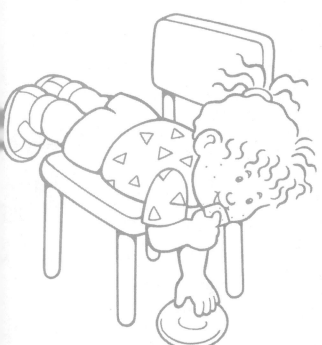

Circulation

Plugged   *I Wonder . . . Why Do I Get Scabs?*   **52**

Big-Hearted   *I Wonder . . . How Big Is My Heart?*   **56**

Lub-Dub   *I Wonder . . . How Does My Heart Sound?*   **60**

Pumper   *I Wonder . . . How Does Blood Move Through My Body?*   **64**

Respiration

In and Out   *I Wonder . . . Why Does My Chest Move When I Breathe?*   **70**

Filled   *I Wonder . . . How Much Breath Do I Have?*   **74**

Frosty   *I Wonder . . . Why Can I See My Breath When It's Cold?*   **78**

Sprays   *I Wonder . . . How Do I Catch a Cold?*   **82**

Squealer   *I Wonder . . . How Do I Talk?*   **86**

Digestion

Choppers   *I Wonder . . . Why Do I Have Different-Shaped Teeth?*   **92**

Squeezed   *I Wonder . . . Can I Swallow Upside Down?*   **96**

Tube Chute   *I Wonder . . . Where Does the Food I Eat Go?*   **100**

Senses

Big and Little   *I Wonder . . . Why Do My Eyes Look Red in Some Photos?*   **106**

Tasty   *I Wonder . . . Why Do Foods Taste Different?*   **110**

Appendix   **Section Summaries**   **114**

Glossary   **119**

Index   **121**

A Letter from Janice VanCleave

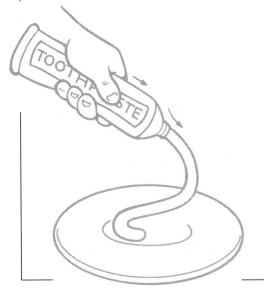

Dear Friends,

Welcome to science playtime!

The scientific play activities in this book are about the human body. Young children are generally curious about their bodies and want to know how they work. Your child will be excited about activities such as making a rubbery bone and a working model of a lung.

Discovering things on their own gives kids a wonderful feeling of success. All they need is your friendly guidance, a few good ideas, and their natural curiosity. This book is full of fun ideas. It contains instructions for more than 50 simple, hands-on experiments inspired by questions from real kids. While you play together, your child will find out the answer to questions such as "Where does the food I eat go?" "Why do I get scabs?" and lots of other things that children wonder about.

So get ready to enter into a science adventure.

Playfully yours,

Janice VanCleave

Before You Begin

1 ***Read the experiment completely before starting.*** When possible, practice doing the experiment by yourself prior to your science playtime. This increases your understanding of the topic and makes you more familiar with the procedure and the materials. If you know the experiment well, it will be easier for you to give instructions and answer questions. If you want to know more about the basic science behind the experiment, see the Appendix.

2 ***Select a place to work.*** The kitchen table is usually the best place for the activities. It provides space and access to an often needed water supply.

3 ***Choose a time.*** There is no best time to play with your child, and play should be the main point when doing the experiments in this book. Select a time when you will have the fewest distractions so that you can complete the experiment. If your family has a schedule, you may allot a specific amount of time for the experiment. You may want to set an exact starting time so that the child can watch the clock and become more familiar with time. Try to schedule 5 to 10 minutes at the close of each session to have everyone clean up.

4 ***Collect supplies.*** You will have less frustration and more fun if all the materials are ready before you start. If food items are to be eaten, hands and supplies must be clean.

5 **Do not rush through the experiment.** Follow each step carefully, and for sure and safe results, never skip steps or add your own. Safety is of the utmost importance, and it is a good science technique to teach children to follow instructions when doing a science experiment.

6 **Have fun!** Don't worry if your child isn't "getting" the scientific principle, or if the results aren't exactly perfect. If you feel the results are too different from those described, reread the instructions and start over from step 1.

7 **Enjoy the wonder of participating in the learning process.** Remember, it is OK for your child not to discover the scientific explanation. For example, when you perform the experiment "Puckered," the child may be too excited about watching "mock skin" pucker to stop and listen to your explanation about why some areas of skin absorb water. Don't force the child to listen. Join in the fun and make a magic moment to remember. Later, when questions arise about why fingers and toes wrinkle after swimming or taking a long bath, you can remind your child of the fun time that you had doing the "Puckered" experiment. Then you can repeat the experiment, providing the explanation.

Tips on Materials

- Some experiments call for water. If you want everything to be at the worktable, you can supply water in a pitcher or soda bottle.

- Extra paper towels are always handy for accidental spills, especially if the experiment calls for liquids. A large bowl can be used for waste liquids, and the bowl can be emptied in the sink later.

- To save time, you can precut some of the materials (except string; see below).

- Do not cut string in advance, because it generally gets tangled and is difficult to separate. You and your child can measure and cut the string together.

- You may want to keep labeled shoe boxes filled with basic supplies that are used in many experiments, such as scissors, tape, and marking pens.

- The specific sizes and types of containers listed in the material lists are those used when these experiments were tested. This doesn't mean that substituting a different type of container will result in an experimental failure. Substitution of supplies should be a value judgment made after you read an experiment to determine the use of the supplies. For example, you could replace an 8-inch (20-cm) circle of white paper with a round coffee filter that is equal, or nearly equal, to 8 inches (20 cm).

- For large groups, multiply the supplies by the number in the group so that each person can perform the experiment individually. Some of the supplies (glue, for instance) can be shared, so read the procedure to determine this ahead of time.

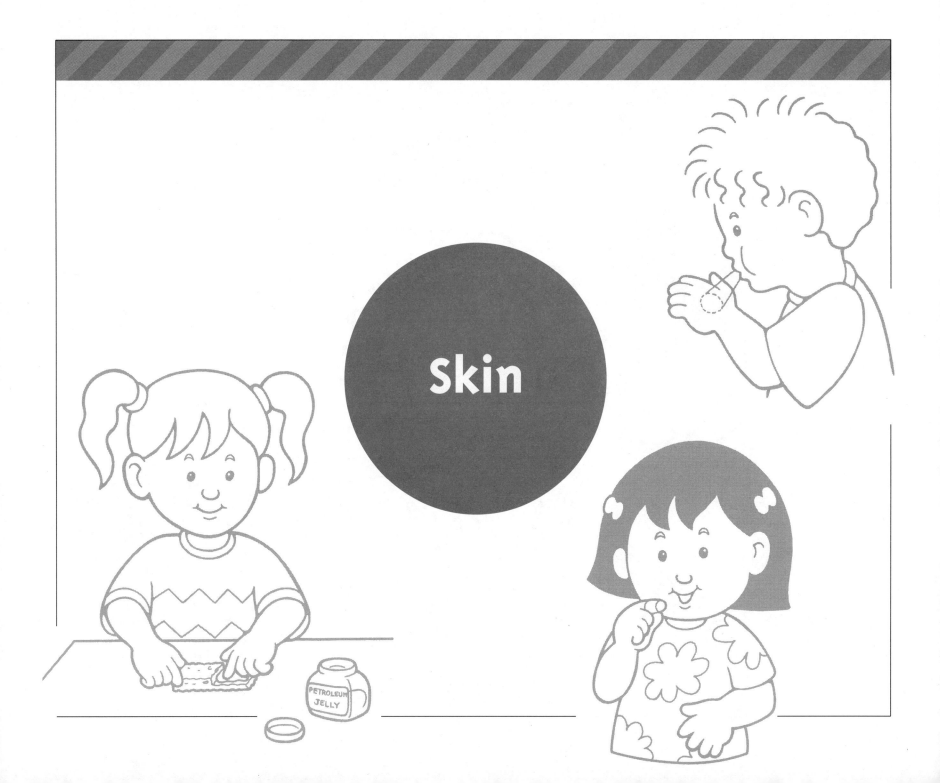

Skin

Ridged

Round Up These Things

dime
transparent tape

Later You'll Need

pencil
2 unruled index cards
transparent tape
magnifying lens

1 Lay the dime on a table.

2 With the tape, cover the tips of the thumb and pointer finger of one of your hands.

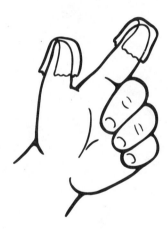

3 With your taped finger-tips, try to pick up the dime. It will be difficult and you may not be able to do it.

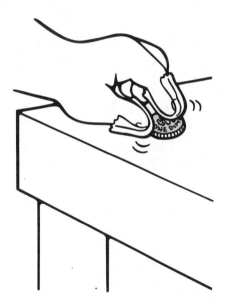

4 Remove the tape from your fingertips and again try to pick up the dime. Now it's easy to do.

So Now We Know

Your fingertips have ridges that make it easier to pick things up. The ridges gripped the coin so it didn't slip out of your fingers.

More Fun Things to Know and Do

Your fingertip ridges make up a special design that is called your fingerprint. You are the only one who has that particular design. Here's a way to collect and study your fingerprints:

- Rub the lead of a pencil back and forth across one of the index cards.

- Rub one fingertip across the pencil marking.

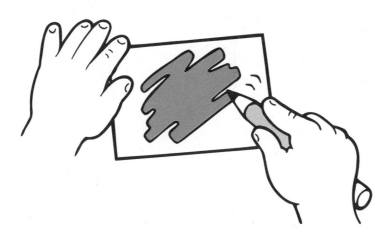

- Cover the smudged fingertip with a piece of transparent tape. Press the tape firmly against your fingertip.

- Carefully remove the tape and press the sticky side against the other index card.

- Use the magnifying lens to study the print.

Even though no one else has exactly the same fingerprint as you, there are basic types of fingerprints. Use the diagram of basic fingerprint patterns to identify your type.

BASIC FINGERPRINT PATTERNS

whorl   loop   arch

Pleated

I wonder . . . Why are my elbows wrinkly?

Let's find out!

Round Up These Things

flexible drinking straw

Later You'll Need

water-soluble black felt-tip pen

II

1 Try to bend the straw where it is not wrinkled. It is difficult to bend.

2 Try to bend the straw where it is wrinkled. The wrinkles stretch out and the straw bends easily.

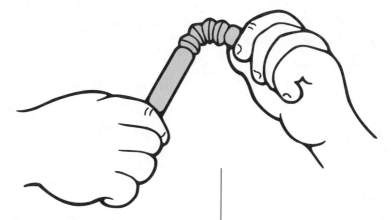

So Now We Know

The skin at your elbows has large wrinkles like the straw. These wrinkles let you bend your arm easily. The skin at other places in your body that bend, such as your knees, toes, and fingers, also has large wrinkles.

More Fun Things to Know and Do

Look at the skin around the parts of your body that bend, such as your knees, toes, and fingers. Here's a way to show off some wrinkles:

- With the felt-tip pen, draw a caterpillar on the underside of your finger as shown.

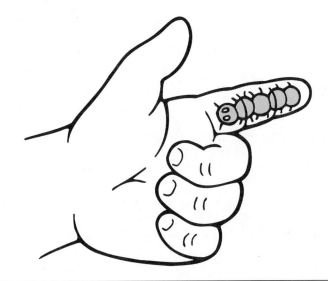

- **Bend and stretch your finger. When you bend your finger, part of the caterpillar disappears in the wrinkled skin. When you stretch your finger, the skin smoothes out and all of the caterpillar can be seen.**

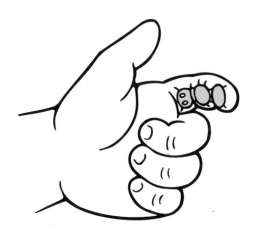

Puckered

Round Up These Things

new cellulose kitchen
  sponge
bowl of tap water
scissors
ruler
petroleum jelly

Later You'll Need

bowl of tap water
timer

1 Rinse the sponge in the bowl of water and squeeze out as much water as possible.

2 ADULT STEP   Cut a 1-inch (2.5cm)-wide strip from the sponge. Keep the strip.

3 ADULT STEP   Cut a section from the sponge strip so that about half of the sponge is half as thick.

4 Allow the sponge strip to dry thoroughly. This may take several hours.

5 Press on the dry sponge strip with your fingers, making it as flat as possible.

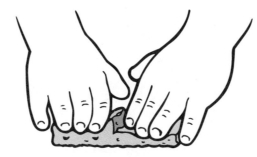

6 Thoroughly cover the surface of the thinner section of the sponge strip with petroleum jelly.

7 Dip your pointer finger into the water in the bowl and hold your wet finger above the part of the sponge coated with petroleum jelly. Allow 2 to 3 water drops to fall onto the sponge. The water drops form round balls that sit on top of the sponge.

 8 Dip your finger again into the water and allow 2 to 3 water drops to fall onto the uncoated part of the sponge. The sponge puckers up where the water falls.

So Now We Know

The skin on the tips of your fingers and toes is different from the rest of your skin. It is thicker, and like the uncoated part of the sponge it is not waterproofed with a coating of oil. That's why it soaks up water and puckers up when you have been in water for a long time.

More Fun Things to Know and Do

Let's see how the rest of your skin keeps out water:

- Dip your finger in the water in the bowl.

- Hold your wet finger above the back of your other hand. Let 2 to 3 drops of water fall onto your hand.

- Observe the water on your skin for 5 to 10 seconds or longer. The water drops sit on your skin and do not sink in.

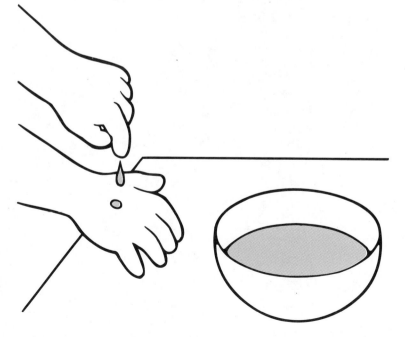

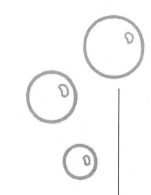

Darker

Round Up These Things

Band-Aid

Later You'll Need

flashlight

① Wrap the Band-Aid around the middle of one finger.

② Leave the Band-Aid on for 2 or more days.

③ Remove the Band-Aid and look at the color of the skin over the entire finger. The skin that was covered by the Band-Aid is much lighter than the rest of your skin.

So Now We Know

A colored substance in your skin called melanin makes your skin dark. When you're in sunlight, more melanin is produced and your skin turns darker, or tans. When sunlight is shut out by a Band-Aid, less melanin is produced. So your skin under the Band-Aid, where the sun couldn't reach, is lighter.

More Fun Things to Know and Do

Your skin also has a rosy tint to it because of the blood underneath the skin. This red coloring is most noticeable in light skin. Even if your skin is very dark, you can see the rosy color of blood in the skin of the palm of your hand. Try this to make the rosy color even easier to see:

- Turn on the flashlight.

- Darken the room.

- Cup your fingers over the bulb end of the flashlight.

- Move your cupped hand around and observe the rosy-colored light that passes through the skin of your fingers.

Keeping Cool

Round Up These Things

ruler
paper towel
tap water

Later You'll Need

large bowl
warm tap water
timer

1 Hold your right hand about 4 inches (10 cm) from your mouth.

2 Blow your breath across the back of your hand. Does your skin feel cooler where you blow on it?

3 Moisten the paper towel with water.

4 Rub the towel over the surface of the back of your right hand.

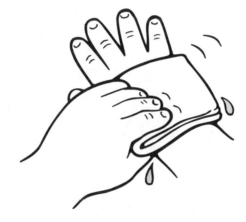

5 Hold the moistened hand about 4 inches (10 cm) from your mouth.

6 Again, blow your breath across the back of your hand. The wet skin feels even cooler where you blow on it.

So Now We Know

When it's hot, you sweat to cool your body off. Sweat is mostly water, which cools your skin as it dries.

More Fun Things to Know and Do

Another way your body cools off is by bringing your blood closer to the surface of your skin. Blood near the skin loses heat. The cooled blood then moves through your body, cooling everything off. Try this to see how your blood comes to the surface:

- Fill the bowl about three-fourths full with warm tap water.

- Soak one hand in the bowl of water for about 1 minute.

- Remove your hand and compare the color of the skin on the soaked hand with that of the dry hand. The soaked hand will be redder because of the blood near the surface.

Hair

Hairy

I wonder . . . Why do I have hair on my body?

Let's find out!

Round Up These Things

box, at least 2 inches (5 cm) taller and wider than a 1-quart (1-liter) jar
cotton balls
two 1-quart (1-liter) jars with lids
2-cup (500-ml) measuring cup
tap water
2 bulb-type thermometers
timer

Later You'll Need

newspaper
art paintbrush with hair bristles
container of powder, such as baby powder
ruler

1 Cover the bottom of the box with a layer of cotton balls.

2 Set one jar in the box. Leave the other jar on the table.

3 Fill the box with cotton balls up to the top of the jar.

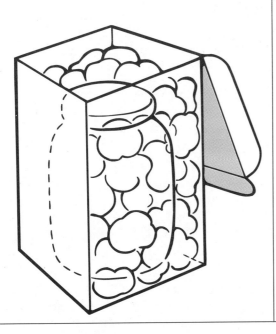

4 ADULT STEP   Use the measuring cup to add 2 cups (500 ml) of hot tap water to each jar.

5 Stand a thermometer in each jar of hot water.

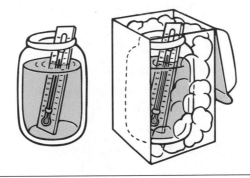

6 After 1 minute, remove the thermometers and compare the height of the liquid in each. The heights are the same or nearly the same.

7 Seal each jar with a lid.

8 Quickly cover the jar in the box with a layer of cotton balls and close the lid on the box.

9 Set the timer for 10 minutes.

10 At the end of 10 minutes, uncover the jars and stand a thermometer in each jar.

11 After 1 minute, remove the thermometers and again compare the height of the liquid in each thermometer. The thermometer's liquid in the jar surrounded by the cotton balls is higher. This means the water in this jar is warmer.

So Now We Know

Hair on your body helps to keep heat from leaving your body the same way the cotton balls helped to keep heat from leaving the water.

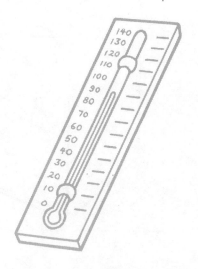

More Fun Things to Know and Do

You have hair in your nose and ears. There is also hair above your eyes, called eyebrows, and on your eyelids, called eyelashes. Small dust and dirt specks stick to these hairs and help keep the specks from entering your nose, ears, and eyes. Here's a way to see how things stick to hair:

- Spread the newspaper on a table.

- Look at the bristles on the art brush. They should be clean.

- Hold the art brush above the newspaper.

- Ask your helper to hold the container of powder so that its open end is about 12 inches (30 cm) from the art brush. Then, spray the powder toward the brush by squeezing the container.

- Again look at the bristles on the brush. Powder sticks to the hairs on the brush.

Curly

Round Up These Things

scissors
ruler
sheet of typing paper

Later You'll Need

straw in a paper wrapper
cup
tap water

1 Cut a 1-by-6-inch (2.5-by-15-cm) strip of paper.

2 Hold the ends of the paper in your hands.

3 Place the strip of paper on the table with one end over the edge.

4 Press the paper tightly against the edge of the table. Keeping the paper taut, pull down on the paper, sliding the entire strip across the table edge.

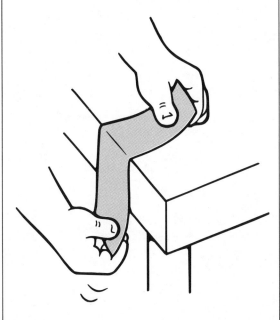

5 Hold one end of the paper. The paper curls up.

So Now We Know

Strands of curly hair bend around. Rubbing the paper in the experiment bent the paper, so it curled up.

More Fun Things to Know and Do

Moist air can make hair twist and bend. Here's a way to see how water changes the shape of hair:

- Stand the paper-wrapped straw on a table and push the paper wrapper down around the straw until the wrapper is as squashed as possible.

- Take the squashed wrapper off the straw and put it on the table.

- Fill the cup half full with water.

- Dip your finger in the water. Use your finger to put 1 drop of water on a section of the wrapper. Dip your finger in the water again and put a drop of water on another section of the wrapper.

- Watch the wrapper twist and bend.

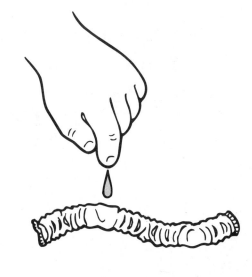

Painless

I wonder . . . Why doesn't my hair hurt when it gets cut?

Let's find out!

Round Up These Things

yourself
scissors

Later You'll Need

yourself

① **ADULT STEP** **Hold one strand of hair on the child's head.**

② **ADULT STEP** **Notify the child when you are ready to cut the end of the hair, then use the scissors to cut the end of the hair.**

③ **With your fingers, hold several strands of hair close to your scalp. Gently pull your hair upward. Do not pull hard enough to jerk the hair out.**

So Now We Know

It did not hurt to cut the end of the hair off, but pulling your hair did hurt. This is because the part of the hair beneath your scalp is alive and can send pain messages to your brain. The hair growing out of the scalp is dead, so the cut end cannot send pain messages.

More Fun Things to Know and Do

You can feel if any hair is touched. Here's a way to test the sensitivity of the hair on your arms:

- Sit in a chair with your arm resting on a table.

- **Turn your head away and close your eyes while someone very gently moves one finger back and forth against the ends of the hairs on your arm. Can you feel the movement?**

Skeleton

Movable

I wonder ...
How does my back bend?

Let's find out!

Round Up These Things

6 thread spools
4-by-5 inch (10-by-
12.5 cm) poster board
pencil
scissors
one-hole paper punch
12-inch (30-cm) piece
of string
transparent tape
ruler

Later You'll Need

sheet of typing paper
masking tape
book
pencil

1 Place the flat end of a thread spool on the poster board.

2 Draw five circles on the poster board by tracing around the end of the spool.

3 Cut out the five circles and use the paper punch to make a hole in the center of each circle.

4 Thread one end of the string through the hole in one of the spools, then tape the end of the string to the end of the spool.

5 Stand the spool on end and thread the free end of the string through the hole in one of the poster board circles. Continue to add spools and circles to the string until all are used. Then,

tape the end of the string to the top spool.

6 Holding the bottom spool on a table, push the top spool about 2 inches (5 cm) to one side.

7 Push the spool in different directions.

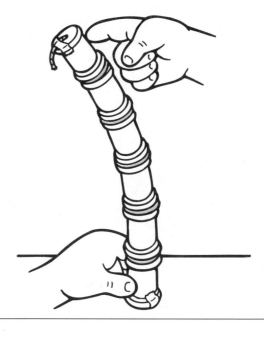

So Now We Know

Your backbone is made of separate bones called vertebrae. When you bend, your vertebrae, like the spools, separate a little so your back can move. Each vertebra has a hole through its back part through which the spinal cord is threaded. Between each vertebra is a pad, like the circle, called a disk. Disks keep the vertebrae from rubbing against each other.

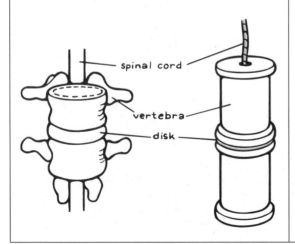

More Fun Things to Know and Do

You are taller in the morning than you are at night. This is because your vertebrae separate during the night when you are lying down, but gravity pulls them together during the day when you stand or sit up. Here's a way to see how much your height changes from morning to evening:

- On the day before the experiment, hold a sheet of paper to the wall so that the top of your head is about even with the middle of the paper.

- Tape the paper to the wall.

- The next morning, as soon as you wake up, measure your height by standing against the wall with your head against the paper. Stand as straight as possible.

- Ask your helper to place a book on your head as in the diagram.

- Ask your helper to make a mark on the paper where the bottom of the book touches the paper. Write MORNING next to the mark.

- In the evening of that same day, measure your height again. Write EVENING next to the mark.

- Compare the morning and evening marks. The morning mark will be a little higher than the evening mark.

Rubbery

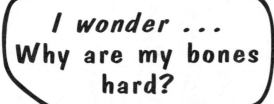

I wonder ... Why are my bones hard?

Let's find out!

Round Up These Things

knife (to be used only by an adult)
cooked chicken leg
dishwashing liquid
1-quart (1-liter) jar with lid
3 cups (750 ml) white vinegar
tongs
NOTE: Wash your hands each time after handling the chicken bone.

Later You'll Need

sheet of typing paper
transparent tape
this book

1 ADULT STEP Cut as much of the meat off the bone as possible.

2 Wash the bone in soapy water and rinse.

3 Try to bend the leg bone with your fingers.

4 Place the bone in the jar.

5 Add the vinegar to the jar.

6 Secure the lid on the jar.

7 After 24 hours, remove the lid. Use the tongs to remove the bone from the jar.

8 Rinse the vinegar off the bone with water.

9 Try bending the bone again.

10 Replace the bone in the jar of vinegar and secure the lid.

11 Repeat steps 7 through 10 each day for 7 or more days. The bone will gradually become easier to bend.

So Now We Know

Bones are hard because they contain a chemical called calcium. The vinegar removes the calcium in the bone, making the bone rubbery. If you didn't have calcium in your bones, you wouldn't be able to stand or move your body.

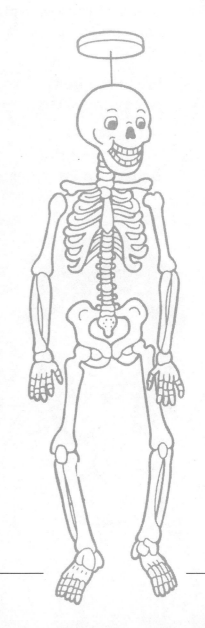

More Fun Things to Know and Do

The long bone in your leg, called your thigh bone, is shaped much like the chicken leg bone. Both have a hollow, cylinderlike shape, which means they're shaped like a tall soup can. Here's a way to make a model of your thigh bone to see how its shape makes it strong:

- Roll the paper into a tube, overlapping the top and bottom edges.

- Tape the ends together as shown.

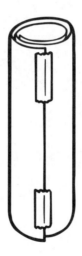

- Stand the tube on a table and lay this book on top of the tube. The paper tube is strong enough to support the weight of the book.

Bendable

I wonder . . . Why do my arms bend?

Let's find out!

Round Up These Things

small box with lid
masking tape

Later You'll Need

adhesive tape

1 Place the box and the lid together on a table with their open sides down.

2 Connect the box and the lid with two strips of tape as shown.

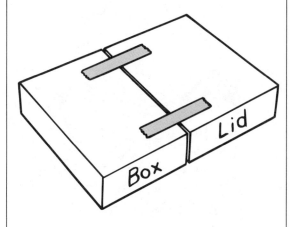

3 Hold the box with one hand and raise the lid with your other hand.

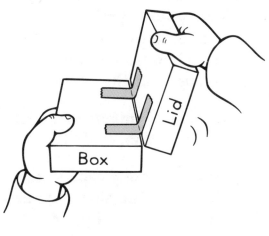

4 Hold the box with one hand and the lid with the other hand. Try to bend the lid down.

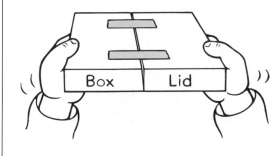

So Now We Know

Your arms bend at your elbows. Your elbow is a joint, which is a place where bones come together. The box represents the bone in your upper arm and the lid represents the bone in your lower arm. The tape pieces are ligaments that hold bones together. An elbow joint, like the box joint you made, is an example of a hinge joint, which can only bend in one direction.

More Fun Things to Know and Do

Your thumb joints allow you to move your thumbs in many directions. Here's a way to demonstrate how important your thumb is:

- Hold your fingers straight and together.

- Have someone tape your thumb to the side of your hand on each of your hands. The end of the thumb must be covered with the tape. Wrap the tape around your hands.

- Try to do such things as picking up objects and eating with your thumbs taped down.

Circulation

Plugged

Round Up These Things

jar, ½ pint (250 ml) or smaller (the smaller the mouth, the better)
tap water
scissors
cheesecloth
rubber band
large bowl

Later You'll Need

3 to 4 purple grapes
paper towel
resealable plastic bag

1 Fill the jar about half full with water.

2 Cut three squares from the cheesecloth large enough to cover the mouth of the jar.

3 Lay the cloth squares one at a time across the mouth of the jar. Position the cloth squares so that the threads crisscross, forming small openings between them.

4 Put the rubber band over the cloth and around the neck of the jar so that the rubber band holds the cloth squares securely against the jar.

5 Set the bowl on a table.

6 Hold the jar upright over the bowl, then quickly turn the jar upside down. At first, some of the water will pour out of the jar, but most of it will stay inside.

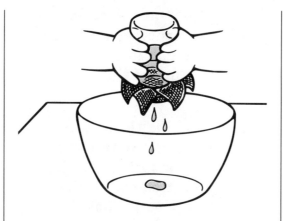

So Now We Know

Water fills the holes between the overlapped threads and stops the water from flowing out of the jar. When you cut yourself, tiny, sticky, thread-like materials in the blood cover the hole and trap the blood. This stops the bleeding. At the surface, the trapped blood and the threadlike materials dry and make a hard scab.

More Fun Things to Know and Do

When you hit yourself on something hard, you may develop a bruise. A bruise shows up because the skin is not broken, but blood vessels underneath the skin are. The blood leaks out under the skin. Here's how to make a model showing the formation of a bruise:

- Wrap the grapes in the paper towel.

- Place the towel inside the plastic bag.

- Lay the bag on a table and hit the bag with your hand so that the grapes break. The juice will spread through the fibers of the paper towel without leaking out of the bag. Think of the plastic bag as your skin, the towel as your body under your skin, the grape as a blood vessel, and the grape juice as blood.

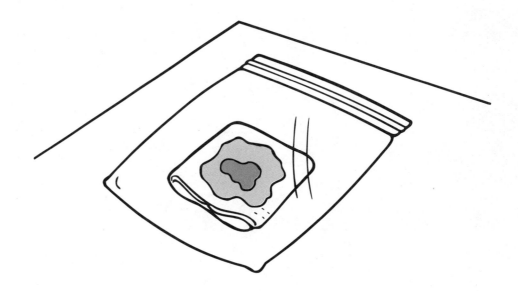

Big-Hearted

Round Up These Things

yourself

Later You'll Need

sheet of typing paper
pencil
crayons

1 Make a fist with your left hand as shown.

2 Hold your fist in the center of your chest.

So Now We Know

Your heart is about as big as your fist. Your heart is wider at the top and more pointed at the bottom. It lies in the center of your chest with its bottom tilted a little toward the left side of your chest.

More Fun Things to Know and Do

A valentine is called a heart, but your heart is not shaped like a valentine. Instead, it is shaped more like an upside-down pear. Look at the shape of a pear shown here and make a drawing of a person with a pear-shaped heart. Don't forget to tilt the bottom a little toward the left side of the chest.

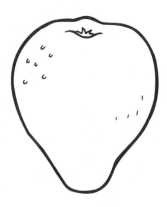

Valentine

Lub-Dub

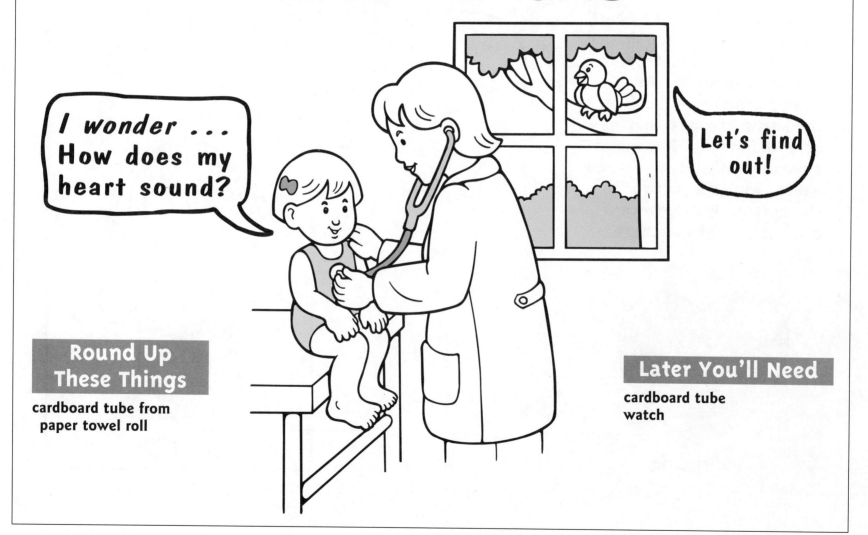

Round Up These Things

cardboard tube from
paper towel roll

Later You'll Need

cardboard tube
watch

1 In a quiet room, ask your helper to hold the paper tube against the center of his or her chest.

2 Place one of your ears over the other end of the tube.

3 Stand very still and listen to the sound of your helper's heart.

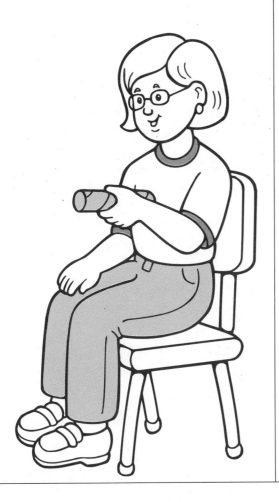

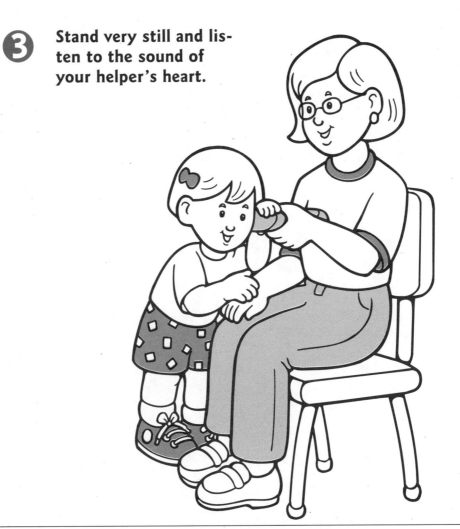

So Now We Know

Your helper's heart made a "lub-dub" sound. Your doctor uses a stethoscope to listen to people's hearts. Your paper tube acts like a stethoscope to make the heartbeat sound louder.

More Fun Things to Know and Do

Each time your heart beats, it pumps blood through your body. Blood carries nutrients and oxygen to all parts of your body. Nutrients come from the food you eat and oxygen comes from the air you breathe. When you exercise, your body needs more nutrients and oxygen. This means your heart has to pump faster. Here's a way to find out how a heart sounds after exercising:

- Ask your helper to run in place for 1 minute.

- Use your paper stethoscope to listen to your helper's heart. Does it sound louder and faster? Softer and slower?

Pumper

I wonder ... How does blood move through my body?

Let's find out!

tennis ball
watch that counts seconds

3 index cards
pencil
five 1-quart (1-liter) jars
tap water
red food coloring
spoon

1 Hold the tennis ball in one hand.

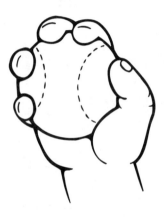

2 Ask your helper to time you while you squeeze the ball for 5 seconds. When your helper says go, start squeezing the ball and try to squeeze the ball eight times before your time is up.

3 When your helper says stop, quit squeezing the ball. Did you squeeze the ball eight times?

So Now We Know

Your heart squeezes about eight times every 5 seconds. The force it takes to squeeze the ball is about the same force needed to squeeze blood out of your heart. Your heart squeezes about 96 times each minute. With every squeeze, the heart pumps blood through the blood vessels in your body. The blood always moves in one direction through the blood vessels as it travels through your body and back to your heart.

More Fun Things to Know and Do

A baby has less blood than a child or an adult. As the baby grows and its body increases in size, the amount of blood also increases. Here's how to show the difference in the amount of blood in a baby, in a child, and in an adult:

- Fold the index cards in half so that they stand up.

- Draw a baby and 1 jar filled with red liquid on one card. Label the card BABY.

- On a second card, draw a child and 3 jars filled with red liquid. Label the card CHILD.

- On a third card, draw an adult and 5 jars filled with red liquid. Label the card ADULT.

- Fill the 1-quart (1-liter) jars with water and add about 10 drops of food coloring to each jar. Stir.

- Stand the card with the baby in front of one jar. This shows about how much blood a baby has—1 quart (1 liter).

- Stand the card with the child in front of 3 jars. This shows about how much blood you have—3 quarts (3 liters).

- Move all the jars together and stand the adult card in front of them. This shows about how much blood adults have—5 quarts (5 liters).

In and Out

I wonder ... Why does my chest move when I breathe?

Let's find out!

Round Up These Things

paper lunch bag

Later You'll Need

scissors
2-liter soda bottle
9-inch (22.5-cm) round balloon
ruler
plastic trash bag
rubber band
Band-Aid

1 Lie on your back.

2 Hold the paper bag over your mouth with one hand and place the other hand on your chest.

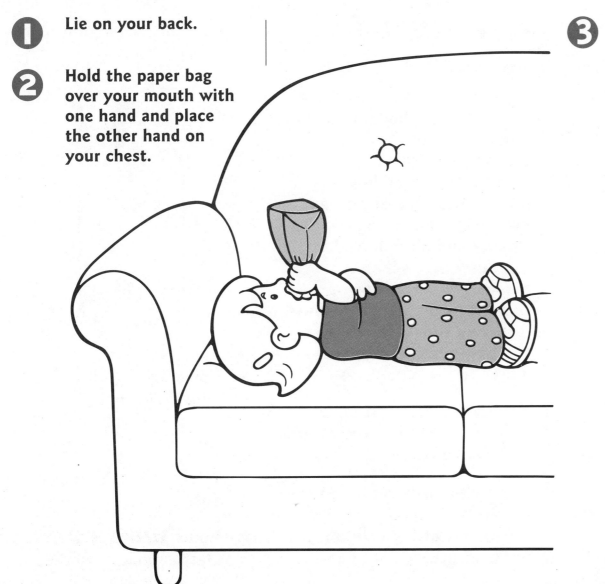

3 Breathe deeply several times. As you breathe, watch the bag and feel your chest. When you breathe in, the bag will empty and your chest will go up. When you breathe out, the bag will fill up and your chest will go down.

So Now We Know

You have two air bags in your chest called lungs that fill with air when you breathe in. When you breathe out, air moves out of your lungs.

More Fun Things to Know and Do

Your chest is like a room with a muscle for a floor. This muscle is called the diaphragm. Your lungs fill most of the space in this room. When the diaphragm moves up, the room gets smaller and air is forced out of your lungs. When the diaphragm moves down, the room is larger and air rushes into your lungs. Here's a way to show how the diaphragm works to fill your lungs:

- ADULT STEP   Cut off and discard the bottom of the soda bottle.

- Put the balloon inside the bottle, stretching the mouth of the balloon over the mouth of the bottle. The balloon represents a lung.

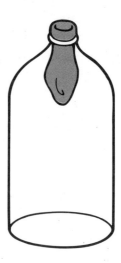

- ADULT STEP   Cut a circle with a 10-inch (25-cm) diameter from the plastic bag.

- Turn the bottle upside down.

- ADULT STEP   Lay the plastic circle over the

cutaway end of the bottle, draw the edges of the plastic around the bottle, and secure the plastic with the rubber band. The plastic represents a diaphragm.

- Stick the ends of the Band-Aid to the middle of the plastic so that it makes a pull tab.

- Hold the bottle upright with one hand and pull the Band-Aid down slightly with the other hand. Notice how the balloon fills up when the plastic diaphragm is pulled down.

- Push the plastic up and watch the balloon deflate.

Filled

I wonder ... How much breath do I have?

Let's find out!

Round Up These Things

2-liter soda bottle
  with lid
tap water
1-gallon (4-liter) bowl
  or pail
flexible drinking straw

Later You'll Need

the same materials
plus
timer
2 to 3 flexible drinking straws

1. Fill the bottle to over-flowing with water and screw on the lid.

2. Fill the bowl about half full with water.

3. **ADULT STEP** Turn the bottle upside down in the bowl of water so that the mouth of the bottle is under water, then take off the lid.

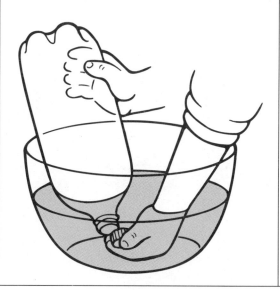

4. Place the short end of the straw into the neck of the bottle.

5. **ADULT STEP** Hold the bottle upside down.

6. Breathe in, then place the straw in your mouth and blow gently into the straw. Do not let the straw come out of the bottle. Remove the straw from your mouth before you breathe in again. All the air that you breathe out collects at the top of the bottle.

So Now We Know

You can see at the top of the bottle how much air you exhale, or breathe out, in one breath.

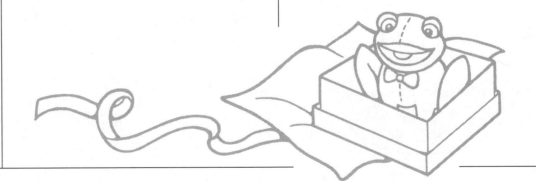

More Fun Things to Know and Do

As you grow, the parts of your body, inside and out, also get bigger. Bigger people have bigger lungs, which hold more air. To show this, ask different-sized people to repeat the previous experiment. Use a clean straw for each person. Compare the amount of air in the bottle after each experiment.

Frosty

I wonder . . . Why can I see my breath when it's cold?

Let's find out!

Round Up These Things

ice cube
resealable plastic sandwich bag
hand mirror

Later You'll Need

drinking straw
1-gallon (4-liter) resealable plastic bag
sheet of black construction paper
desk lamp or window with direct light
magnifying lens

1 Place the ice cube in the plastic bag and seal the bag.

2 Lay the plastic bag on the mirror.

3 Gently press the ice against the mirror and rub it back and forth over the mirror's surface several times to cool the glass.

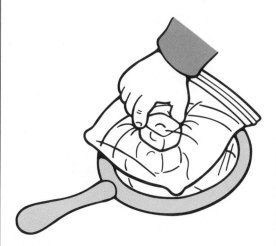

4 Remove the bag of ice and immediately hold the mirror close to, but not touching, your mouth. Exhale on the mirror. The mirror looks foggy.

So Now We Know

Your breath has water in it that you can't see. When you breathe into cold air or on the cold mirror, the water in your breath collects into a cloud of tiny drops of water that you can see.

More Fun Things to Know and Do

You exhale water into the air with each breath you take. Here's another way to see the water you exhale:

- Place the end of the straw in the plastic bag and seal the bag up to the straw.

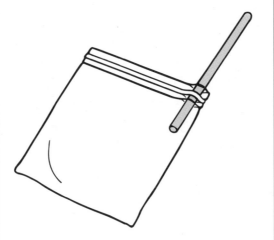

- Take a deep breath, exhale through the straw, then immediately remove the straw from the bag and press the opening of the bag shut.

- Lay the paper on a table near a lamp or window with direct light.

- Place the bag on top of the paper. The inside of the bag is fogged with water from your exhaled breath.

- Look at the bag with the magnifying lens. Different-sized water drops can be seen on the inside of the bag.

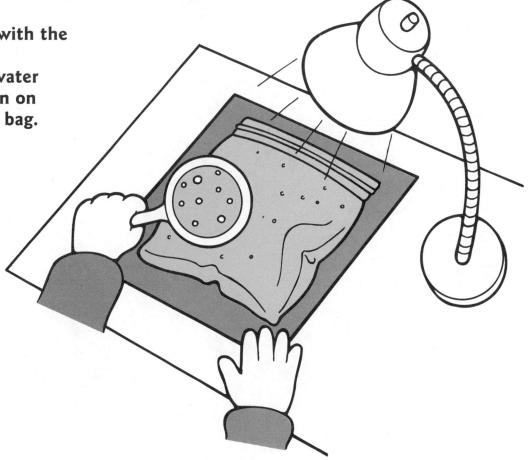

Sprays

Round Up These Things

facial tissue

Later You'll Need

facial tissue
ruler

1 Hold two ends of the facial tissue.

2 Hold the tissue against the end of your nose so that the tissue covers your nose and mouth.

3 Cough and observe the movement of the tissue.

So Now We Know

You catch a cold from germs that are so small they can float in the air. When a person with a cold coughs or sneezes, moist air containing cold germs is sprayed into the air. The tissue blew outward when you coughed into it. If the tissue had not been there, the moist air would have sprayed several yards (meters) away from your body.

More Fun Things to Know and Do

Here's a way to see how far air leaving your mouth can reach:

- Hold the facial tissue about 4 inches (10 cm) in front of your face.

- Cough and observe the movement of the tissue. The bottom of the tissue moves outward.

- Hold the tissue at arm's length from your face.

- Again, cough and observe the movement of the tissue. The tissue moves less at this distance.

Squealer

Round Up These Things

balloon

Later You'll Need

yourself

1 Inflate the balloon and hold the opening closed with your fingers.

2 Hold each side of the neck of the balloon with your fingers and stretch the balloon outward to let the air out a little at a time. The air leaving the balloon makes a squealing sound.

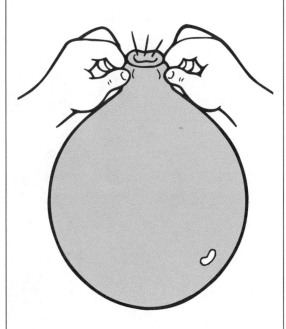

So Now We Know

When you talk, air from your lungs passes through vocal cords in your throat. These cords act like the balloon neck to make different sounds.

More Fun Things to Know and Do

Let's see what would happen if you tried to hum with your mouth and nose closed:

- Hum a tune with your mouth closed.

- As you continue to hum, pinch your nose closed with your fingers.

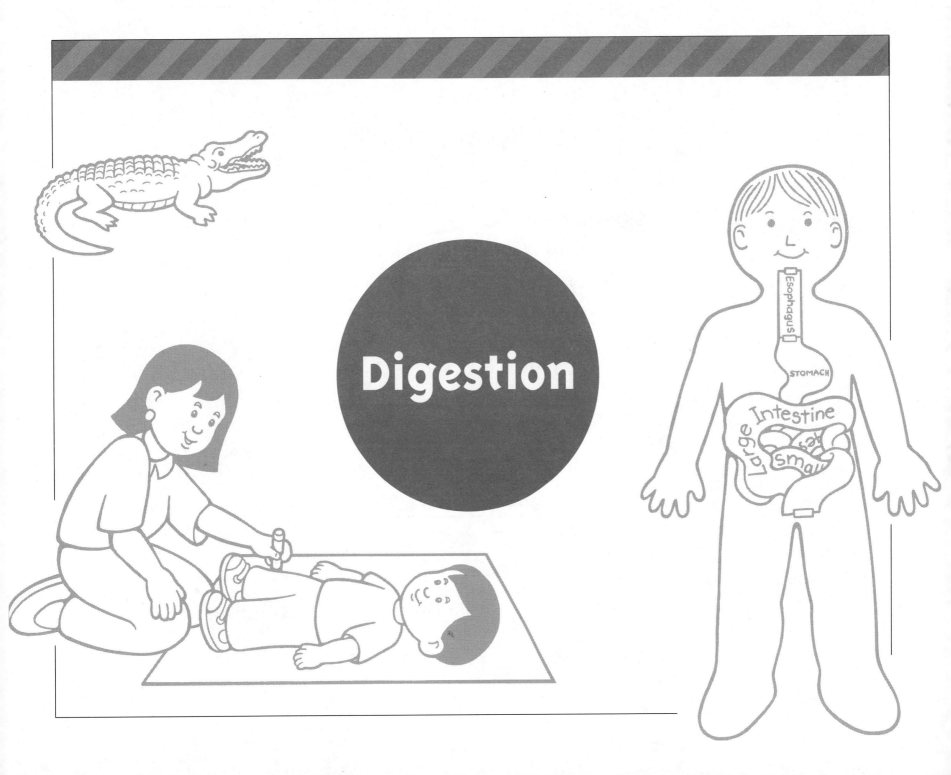

Digestion

Choppers

I wonder ... Why do I have different-shaped teeth?

Let's find out!

Round Up These Things

apple

Later You'll Need

scissors
brown construction paper
small empty box, such as for rice
transparent tape
1-inch (2.5-cm)–wide roll of
  masking tape
serrated knife (to be used only
  by an adult)
marker
crayons

1 Take a bite from the apple using your front teeth.

2 First, try to chew the bite from the apple with your front teeth.

3 Then, chew the piece of apple in your mouth with your back teeth and swallow it.

4 Try to bite the apple with the teeth on the side of your mouth.

5 Chew any piece of apple in your mouth and swallow it.

So Now We Know

Your front teeth are wide and thin at the edges. They are best at biting food and not very good at chewing. The teeth in the back of your mouth have large, uneven top surfaces. These teeth are best at grinding food and not very good at biting.

More Fun Things to Know and Do

Babies are usually born without teeth. By the age of 2, a child usually has 20 teeth, called "milk" teeth or "baby" teeth. Around 6 years of age, the milk teeth begin to be pushed out and replaced by permanent teeth. There are 32 teeth in a full set of adult permanent teeth. Here's how to make a model of milk teeth:

- Cut the paper to fit around the sides of the box.

- Wrap the paper around the sides of the box and secure it with transparent tape.

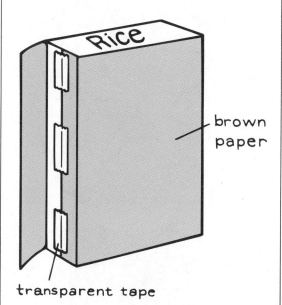

brown paper

transparent tape

- Draw a line around the middle of the box.

- Wrap a strip of masking tape around the box with one edge of the tape along the line drawn around the box. On the opposite side of the line, wrap a second strip of masking tape around the box.

- **ADULT STEP** Use the knife to cut across the box between the strips of masking tape, but stop at one of the narrow sides of the box as shown.

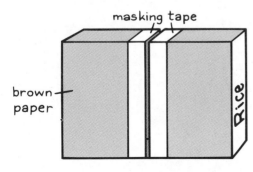

masking tape

brown paper

Rice

- Use the marker to draw 10 teeth on each strip of masking tape. Follow the picture to see which kind of teeth and how many to draw where.

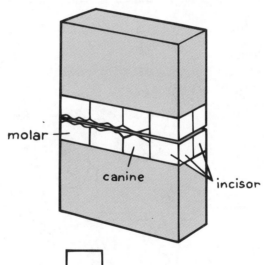

molar

canine

incisor

8 molar (grinding)

4 canine (tearing)

8 incisor (cutting)

- With the scissors, cut out the uneven edges of the molars and the pointed tips of the canine teeth.

- Use the crayons to draw a face on the box for fun. Open and close the bottom of the box to make the model chew.

Squeezed

Round Up These Things

cracker
saucer
chair without arms

Later You'll Need

tube of toothpaste
saucer

1 Place the cracker in the saucer and set the saucer on the floor beside the chair.

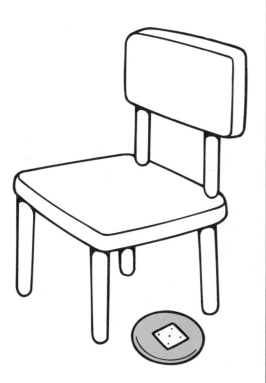

2 Lie across the chair.

3 Take a bite of the cracker, then chew and swallow it.

So Now We Know

You can swallow lying on your stomach. You could even swallow upside down, but it isn't a good idea to try it since you might choke. It's possible to swallow if you aren't standing up, because food doesn't just fall down your throat into your stomach. Your tongue shapes and pushes food into a tube called the esophagus, which squeezes the food into your stomach.

More Fun Things to Know and Do

Here's a way to show how special muscles push food through the esophagus into your stomach:

- Open the tube of tooth-paste and hold the open end over the saucer.

- Squeeze the tube.

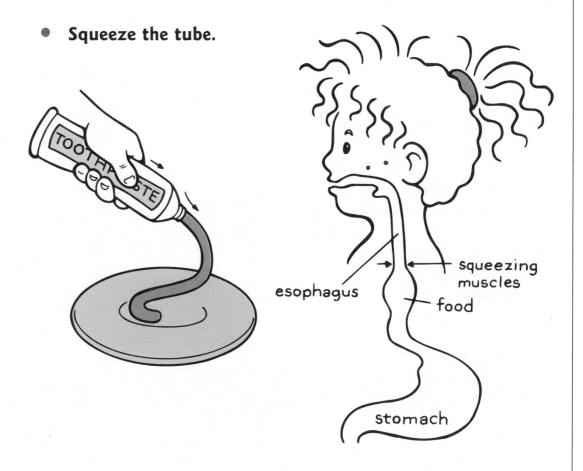

esophagus

squeezing muscles

food

stomach

Tube Chute

I wonder . . . Where does the food I eat go?

Let's find out!

Round Up These Things

ruler
scissors
adding-machine tape
pen
6-inch (15-cm)–square
  piece of white con-
  struction paper
two 9-by-12-inch
  (22.5-by-30-cm)
  sheets of pink con-
  struction paper
masking tape

Later You'll Need

brown butcher or bulletin
  board paper (found at craft
  or teaching supply stores)
scissors
colored markers or crayons

1 Measure and cut two strips of adding-machine tape. Make one 8 inches (20 cm) long and the other 15 feet (4.5 m) long.

2 Label the short paper strip ESOPHAGUS and the long one SMALL INTESTINE.

3 Use the pen to draw a stomach and label it STOMACH on the white piece of construction paper. Follow the picture to see the size and general shape of the stomach. Make widths A and B on the picture equal to the width of the adding-machine tape.

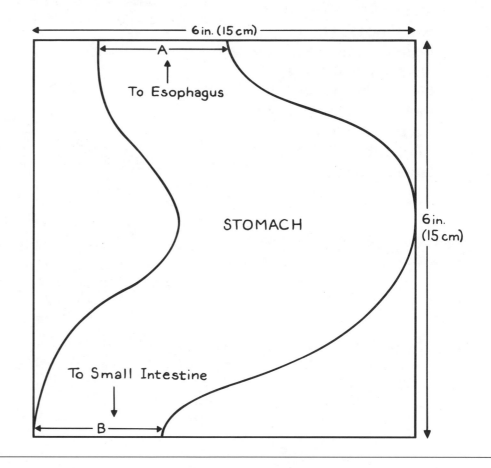

4 Cut out the drawing of the stomach.

5 Cut the 2 sheets of pink construction paper in half lengthwise. Make a long strip that is 4½ inches (11.25 cm) wide by overlapping the short ends of the 4 pieces of paper about ½ inch (1.25 cm) and connecting them with tape. Label this strip large intestine.

| Large | Intestine |

6 Tape the pieces of your model together in this order: esophagus, stomach, small intestine, and large intestine. Stretch the paper sheets out as straight as possible on the floor.

So Now We Know

You have made a model of your digestive tubes. These tubes are the path that the food you swallow takes through your body.

More Fun Things to Know and Do

Your digestive tubes are longer than your body is tall, so how do they fit inside your body? Here's how to make a model of your body showing how everything fits:

- Lie on a piece of butcher paper and ask a helper to draw around your body.

- Cut out the tracing.

- Lay out the digestive tubes on the paper as in the diagram. The esophagus starts under the chin, the stomach lies under the esophagus, and the intestines are wrapped around to fit in the belly.

- For fun, use the colored markers to complete the drawing by adding a face and hair.

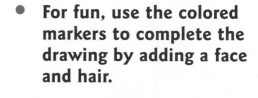

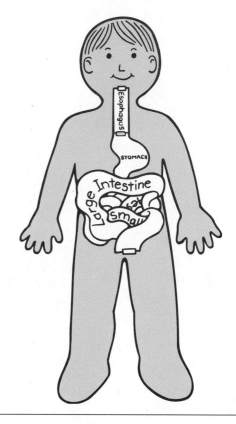

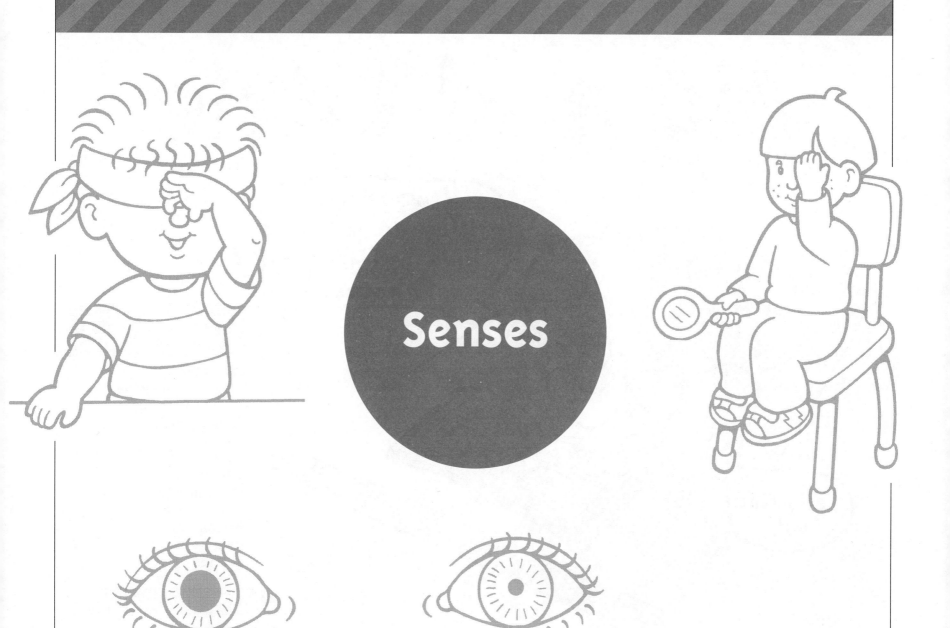

Senses

Big and Little

I wonder ... Why do my eyes look red in some photos?

Let's find out!

Round Up These Things

cereal bowl
sheet of typing paper
pencil
drinking glass
crayons
dime
scissors
aluminum foil
rubber band
flashlight
ruler
quarter

Later You'll Need

hand mirror
watch

1 Place the bowl upside down in the center of the paper.

2 Use the pencil to draw around the outside of the bowl.

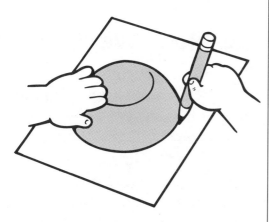

3 Turn the glass upside down in the center of the circle and draw around the outside of the glass.

4 Use a crayon to color the inside circle the same color as your eyes.

5 Lay the dime in the center of the colored circle and draw around it with the pencil.

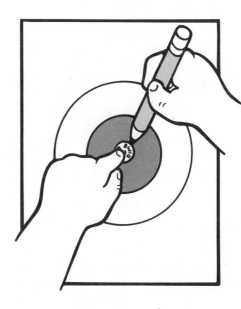

6 ADULT STEP   Cut out the small circle in the center of the paper. The hole represents the black dot in your eye, called the pupil.

7 Line the bowl with aluminum foil.

8 Place the paper over the foil-lined bowl so that the hole in the paper is over the center of the bowl.

---

9 Secure the paper with the rubber band.

9 Secure the paper with the rubber band.

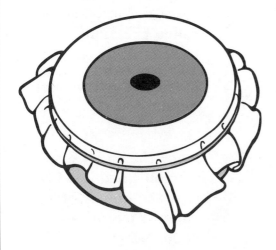

10 Set the bowl on a table and hold the flashlight about 6 inches (15 cm) above the hole in the paper. The light from the flashlight enters the hole in the paper, bounces off the aluminum foil that lines the bowl, and shines back out the hole. Look

at the hole and notice how bright it looks.

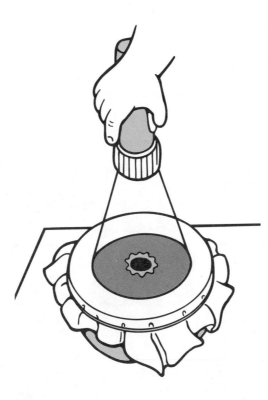

11 Take the paper off the bowl, lay the quarter in the center over the hole, and draw around the quarter.

12 ADULT STEP Cut out the circle on the paper.

13 Repeat steps 8 through 10. Notice that more light bounces out through the larger hole.

So Now We Know

The pupils in your eyes are really holes covered with see-through skin. When you are photographed, the light from the camera's flash enters the eye through your pupil. Some of the light bounces back toward the camera. Your eyes look red in a photo when your pupils are very large. More light is going into your eyes, and more of the light bounces off the red blood vessels in the back of your eye.

More Fun Things to Know and Do

Your pupils get smaller in bright light and larger in the dark. Here's a way to see how light changes the size of your pupils:

- Sit in a brightly lit room or outside in the sunshine. *Caution: Never look directly at the sun because it can permanently damage your eyes.*

- Close one eye and leave the other eye open.

- Cup one hand over the closed eye. Hold a mirror in the other hand.

- Look at the pupil of the open eye in the mirror.

- After 2 to 3 minutes, open the closed eye and quickly look at its pupil in the mirror.

Tasty

Round Up These Things

½ teaspoon (2.5 ml) sugar
½ teaspoon (2.5 ml) salt
½ teaspoon (2.5 ml) unsweetened cocoa powder
½ teaspoon (2.5 ml) lemonade powder
plate
drinking glass
tap water
4 cotton swabs

Later You'll Need

3 different kinds of fruit juice
four 3-ounce (90-ml) paper cups
tap water
scarf that can be used as a blindfold

III

1 Place the sugar, salt, cocoa, and lemonade in separate areas on the plate.

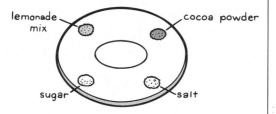

2 Fill the glass with water.

3 Dip a cotton swab in the water, touch it to the sugar in the plate, then lick the swab with your tongue. Discard the swab.

4 Swallow the food and decide if the food tasted sweet, salty, bitter, or sour.

5 Drink some water to wash out the taste of the food.

6 Repeat steps 3 and 4, using the other three foods.

So Now We Know

Your tongue has bumps on it called taste buds. These let your tongue taste things that are sweet, salty, bitter, and sour. The sugar is sweet, the salt is salty, the cocoa is bitter, and the lemonade is sour.

More Fun Things to Know and Do

The taste of food depends not only on your tongue but also on your nose. Here's a way to discover that certain tastes are a combination of flavor and smell:

- So that the tester does not know what juice is being tested, prepare the drinks before the experiment. Pour each fruit juice into a cup. Fill the fourth cup with water.

- Blindfold the tester so that the drinks cannot be identified by sight.

- Instruct the tester to pinch his or her nose closed during the entire experiment. It is important not to sneak a smell during the experiment.

- Hand one cup of juice to the tester and give instructions to drink the juice and identify it.

- After making the identification, have the tester drink some water to wash out the taste of the juice. Repeat the testing procedure for the other two juices.

- Repeat the testing procedure without the tester holding his or her nose.

water

Appendix
Section Summaries

Skin

The protective outer covering on your body is called **skin**. There are two layers of skin, an outer layer called the **epidermis**, and the under layer, called the **dermis**. The boundary between the dermis and the epidermis is not straight and smooth, but consists of small folds. These folds produce a series of ridges and grooves in areas where the skin is thick: the palm of the hand, the sole of the foot, and the fingertips, for example. The patterns formed by the ridges on the fingertip areas are called **fingerprints**. The ridges on the fingertips increase friction. **Friction** is the resistance to motion between two surfaces that are touching each other. The experiment "Ridged" (pages 6–9) shows how the ridges help you to pick up objects. It also shows how to collect and identify fingerprint patterns.

Skin doesn't fit tightly around your entire body. Instead, it is loose at **joints** (a place where two bones come together) to allow movement. The experiment "Pleated" (pages 10–13) shows that there is extra skin around joints, such as the elbows and the knuckles in fingers.

The outer layers of skin are flat, dead cells called **squames**. Squames have a hexagonal (six-sided) shape and overlap each other at the edges, like cards that are shuffled. Flat layers of squames plus natural body oil called **sebum** make most of your skin almost waterproof. But the skin on the tips of your fingers and toes is less waterproof. This skin has many more layers of cells than other parts of your body, but it lacks the **glands** (body parts that produce fluids) that make sebum. Because of its thickness and because it is less water resistant, the skin on your fingers and toes soaks up many times as much water as other skin layers when you stay in water a long time. The swollen squames are too big to lie flat, so the skin wrinkles. The experiment "Puckered" (pages 14–17) models the puckering of the skin on toes and fingers, and shows how waterproof most of your skin is.

Skin is colored in different ways. One way is by special cells in the skin that contain the dark **pigment** (coloring substance) called **melanin**. People with a lot of melanin have dark skin, and those with only a little melanin have light skin. Accumulations of melanin in the skin cause freckles. Exposure to the sun stimulates melanin production. Melanin protects the skin from the sun's burning rays.

The color of oxygen-rich blood is red, and oxygen-poor blood is a bluish red. The oxygen-rich blood in tiny **blood vessels** (tubes that carry blood) called **capillaries** near the surface of the skin adds a rosy hue to skin color. The larger, blue blood vessels visible near the skin's surface are called **veins**. They are blue because they carry oxygen-poor blood. The experiment "Darker" (pages 18–21) shows how melanin and blood give skin color.

One of the jobs of skin is to help maintain a steady internal body temperature of about 98.6°F (37°C). When the temperature of the skin increases, sweat glands produce **sweat**, which is mainly water. When the sweat removes enough heat from your skin, **evaporation** (change of a liquid to a gas) occurs, taking heat away from your body in the process. The **dilation** (enlargement) of capillaries near the skin is another way to keep the body cool. The dilated blood vessels carry more warm blood to the surface, where air touching the skin can cool the blood. This extra blood near the skin is what causes your face to flush when you get hot. The experiment "Keeping Cool" (pages 22–24) shows how evaporation and flushing cool the body.

Hair

Strands of hair trap air between them. The hair and the trapped air are **insulators** (materials that slow down the transfer of energy such as heat). Hair on the body also acts as a collector to prevent foreign materials from entering the body through the nose, ears,

and eyes. The experiment "Hairy" (pages 26–29) demonstrates that hair protects the body from losing heat and shows how hair traps airborne particles.

Hair is straight, wavy, or curly because of its shape. A cross section of a strand of straight hair shows that it has the most rounded shape. The flatter the cross section, the curlier the hair strand. High **humidity** (water in air) causes hair to change shape. This is because parts of the hair strand absorb water and get fatter. This makes the hair twist and bend in different directions. Some curly hair gets straighter, and other curly hair gets curlier. Some straight hair may get slightly curly. The experiment "Curly" (pages 30–33) uses models to show why hair curls.

Ads often claim that certain shampoos and conditioners make hair come "alive," but the truth is that the hair that grows outside your body is dead. The part of each hair beneath the skin is alive, but it dies before it ever reaches the surface of the skin. The experiment "Painless" (pages 34–37) shows that the dead hair doesn't feel anything, but that the hair under the skin is connected to **nerves** (special fibers that the body uses to send messages to and

from the brain or spinal cord) that are very sensitive. Dead hair cannot feel a touch, but it moves the nerve under the skin that sends a message telling your brain that the hair has been touched.

Skeleton

All the bones of your body make up the **skeletal system**. This system provides the framework that allows you to stand upright and protects delicate internal body parts. A baby has more than 300 bones, but some of the bones eventually join together. An adult has about 206 bones.

The central support for your entire body is your **spine** (backbone). It is made up of 26 linked bones, called **vertebrae**, which become progressively larger down your back. Through the back of the vertebrae is a bundle of nerves called the **spinal cord**. You are able to bend because your vertebrae are separated. The disks between the vertebrae keep the bones from grinding together. The experiment "Movable" (pages 40–43) uses a model to show how flexible the backbone is. It also demonstrates that you are taller in the morning. This is because, during the night, the liquid-filled disks and the vertebrae separate. Standing squeezes out liquid in the disks because **gravity** (a force that pulls things toward the center of the earth) pulls the vertebrae together.

The hard part of bones is made up mainly of the chemical **calcium phosphate.** Fibers called **collagen** run through the calcium phosphate. Calcium phosphate gives bones firmness and strength, and collagen gives them flexibility. The experiment "Rubbery" (pages 44–47) shows how to remove calcium from a bone, leaving the rubbery collagen. Eating things with vinegar will not make your bones rubbery. Your body's bones are not soaked in the vinegar. This experiment also shows how the shape of your thigh bone gives it strength. The hollow, cylindrical or can shape of some bones not only increases their strength, but makes them lightweight.

Bones are held together by tough, straplike strands of connective material called **ligaments**. No one is "double-jointed," but people can have extra long ligaments at different joints, allowing them to bend farther than usual. The body needs joints in order to be able to bend, turn, and twist. The experiment "Bendable" (pages 48–50) shows how the elbow bends.

Circulation

When the skin is cut, blood vessels are usually cut. Blood flows out of the cut vessel until small blood cells rush to the wound. (**Cells** are basic body units.) These cells, called **platelets**, help to form the threadlike fibers that make a web at the wound opening. Blood is trapped in the webbing and forms a **clot** (a lump that forms in a liquid). The clot dries and hardens into a crust called a **scab** and the wound is closed. If you pull a scab off, the wound can start bleeding again.

A **bruise** is an injury in which the skin is discolored but not broken. The discoloration is due to blood that leaks out broken blood vessels into **tissue** (groups of similar cells that form various body parts) beneath the skin. The color of the bruise changes because of special blood cells called **phagocytes**. The job of phagocytes is to keep the inside of the body clean by eating such things as invading **germs** (microscopic organisms that can cause diseases) and spilled blood under the skin. The color of a bruise changes as phagocytes eat the blood cells and chemicals destroy their once-red pigments. The experiment "Plugged" (pages 52–55) models the clotting of blood and bruising.

The human heart does not look like a valentine. Instead it is more pear shaped, with the pointed end leaning toward the left side of the chest. The heart's size and weight change with growth. A baby's heart is smaller and lighter than an adult heart. The experiment "Big-Hearted" (pages 56–59) shows the size and shape of a child's heart.

Heart sounds are the sounds made by the heart's **valves** (flaps of tissue that control the flow of blood or other liquids in the body) as they open and shut. The softer "lub" sound is from the valves shutting in the top chambers of the heart. The louder "dub" sound is from the heart valves shutting off the big vessels leaving the heart. The heart pumps blood to carry nutrients and oxygen to all the cells of your body. **Nutrients** are substances in food that are needed for body growth, repair, and energy. **Oxygen** is a gas in the air that is needed for life. The experiment "Lub-Dub" (pages 60–63) uses a homemade **stethoscope** (an instrument used to listen to sounds made by the body, specifically the heart and lungs) to hear a heartbeat.

The heart pushes blood through blood vessels throughout the body. The oxygen-rich blood moves away from the heart through **arteries**, and the oxygen-poor blood returns to the heart through veins. A child's heart is smaller and beats about 96 times each minute. An adult heart is larger and beats about 70 times each minute. The experiment "Pumper" (pages 64–67) demonstrates how hard the heart works in pushing blood through the blood vessels. It also demonstrates the different quantity of blood in a baby, a child, and an adult.

Respiration

When you breathe in, air moves in through your nose or mouth and down your **trachea** (windpipe) to your lungs. The **diaphragm** (a sheet of muscle that forms the floor of the body's chest) controls your breathing. You **inhale** (breathe in) when the diaphragm moves down. You **exhale** (breathe out) when the diaphragm moves up. The experiment "In and Out" (pages 70–73) shows how you breathe.

Lungs are not completely filled or emptied by normal breathing. Most of the time, during normal breathing adults exhale about 1 pint (0.5 liter) of air in one breath. Children exhale even less. When exercising, adults and chil-dren inhale and exhale more air. The experiment "Filled" (pages 74–77) shows how much air is exhaled by a child and older people.

Your breath forms a small cloud on cold days because it contains water. The cold air makes the water change from a gas to tiny liquid drops. The cloud quickly disappears because the liquid droplets change back into a gas that cannot be seen. In the experiment "Frosty" (pages 78–81), you can see and collect the water in your breath.

Colds are caused by **viruses** (tiny germs that grow in living cells). Cold viruses enter a person's nose or throat cells, multiply, burst the cells, and spread to other cells. They are also spread to other people. Viruses and other germs are also spread when saliva and mucus from your nose get on your hands or other objects. (**Saliva** is a liquid in the mouth and **mucus** is a thick, sticky liquid that moistens the nose, mouth, lungs, and other parts of the body.) The germs are left on everything you touch and can be picked up by another person. Keeping your hands clean and away from your eyes, nose, and mouth helps to stop the spread of germs.

Coughing and sneezing are two of the body's automatic ways of clearing out irritating substances, such as dust, pollen, or mucus, from the airways. Coughing is how the body gets rid of something that irritates the lining of lower airways. Sneezing is the way the body gets rid of irritating particles from the nose. When you cough, air comes mostly out the mouth, and when you sneeze, air comes mostly out the nose. The experiment "Sprays" (pages 82–85) shows ways that germs are spread through the air.

You make sounds when air passes between the vocal cords in your throat and causes them to **vibrate** (move back and forth). **Vocal cords** are two strips of tough, elastic tissue and muscle stretched across the opening of the voice box in your throat. All sounds are produced by the vibration of objects. You use your lips, teeth, tongue, cheeks, and throat muscles to help you shape different sounds into words. In the experiment "Squealer" (pages 86–89), a balloon is used to make sounds.

Digestion

Before food can be used by the body, it must be chopped into small pieces so that it is easier to **digest** (change into a form that can be used by the body). Your teeth chop up your food. Chewing is the first step in the digestion of food. The experiment "Choppers" (pages 92–95) shows the jobs of different-shaped teeth. Children also build a model of teeth.

When you eat, food is chopped and ground by the teeth and mixed with saliva, which softens and partially digests food. Then, your tongue rolls the mixture into a ball. This ball, called a **bolus**, is pushed into the food tube called the **esophagus**. The esophagus leads from the back of the throat to the **stomach** (a pouch where chewed food is further digested). Muscles in the esophagus squeeze the bolus and move it forward. This process of pushing food forward is called **peristalsis**. The experiment "Squeezed" (pages 96–99) shows how food is moved through the esophagus.

The **digestive system** is a group of body parts that break food down into usable nutrients and **waste** (the nonuseful solid part of food that exits the body through the anus; called feces or stool). The **anus** is the opening at the lower end of the large intestine. The experiment "Tube Chute" (pages 100–103) shows the basic parts of the digestive system and their approximate sizes for a child.

Senses

You interact with the world around you through your five basic senses: sight, taste, smell, hearing, and touch. The experiment "Big and Little" (pages 106–109) shows how the **pupil** (black dotlike opening in the colored part of the eye) changes size and thus controls the amount of light entering the eye. White light is made up of the different rainbow colors of light: red, orange, yellow, green, blue, indigo, and violet. These different colors are reflected off objects of the same color. When white light from a camera flash enters the pupil of the eye, the red part of white light reflects off the red blood vessels at the back of the eye. The more dilated the pupil, the more red light reflected off the eyes and the redder the eyes in the photo.

To experience taste, chemicals from food must first dissolve in your mouth's saliva. This liquid then moves into the openings at the top of the **taste buds** (cells on the tongue that identify different tastes) and a taste message is sent to your brain. The experiment "Tasty" (pages 110–113) identifies the four basic tastes. It also shows how smell affects the flavor of foods.

Glossary

anus The opening at the lower end of the large intestine.

arteries Blood vessels that carry oxygen-rich blood away from the heart.

blood vessels Tubes that carry blood in the body.

bolus A food ball prepared in the mouth and swallowed.

bruise An injury in which the skin is discolored but not broken. Discoloration is due to blood released from broken blood vessels into tissue.

calcium phosphate A chemical in bones that gives them firmness and strength.

capillaries Tiny blood vessels.

cells Basic body units.

clot A lump that forms in a liquid.

collagen Fibers of protein such as in bones that give them their flexibility.

dermis The under layer of skin.

diaphragm A sheet of muscle that forms the floor of the body's chest.

digest To change food into a form that can be used by the body.

digestive system The group of body parts that break food down into nutrients.

dilation Enlargement of something, such as blood vessels or eye pupils.

epidermis The outer layer of skin.

esophagus The food tube leading from the back of the throat to the stomach.

evaporation The change of a liquid to a gas.

exhale To breathe out.

fingerprint A pattern formed by the ridges on fingertips.

friction The resistance to motion between two surfaces that are touching each other.

germs Microscopic organisms that can cause diseases.

gland A body part that produces a fluid.

gravity A force that pulls things toward the center of the earth.

humidity Water in air.

inhale To breathe in.

insulator A material that slows down the transfer of energy such as heat.

joint The point where bones come together.

ligaments Tough, straplike strands of connective material that hold bones together.

lungs Air bags in your chest that fill with air when you breathe in.

melanin The dark pigment that gives color to the skin, eyes, and hair.

mucus A thick, sticky liquid that moistens the nose, mouth, lungs, and other parts of the body.

nerves Special fibers that the body uses to send messages to and from the brain or spinal cord.

nutrients Substances in food that are needed for growth, repair, and energy.

oxygen A gas in the air needed for life.

peristalsis The process by which muscles contract and relax to push food forward.

phagocytes Special blood cells that eat germs and other things, such as spilled blood under the skin, to keep the inside of the body clean.

pigment A coloring substance.

platelets Blood cells that form fibers used to clot blood where blood vessels are cut.

pupil The black dotlike opening in the colored part of the eye.

saliva   A liquid in the mouth that softens and partially digests food.

scab   A crust over a wound formed by the drying and hardening of blood clots.

sebum   Natural body oil.

skeletal system   The body's framework, made up of all the bones of the body.

skin   The protective outer covering on the body.

spinal cord   Bundle of nerves running from the brain through the vertebrae of the spine.

spine   Backbone.

squames   Flat, dead cells in the outer skin layers.

stethoscope   An instrument used to listen to the heart and lungs.

stomach   The pouch where chewed and swallowed food goes and is further digested.

sweat   A liquid produced by sweat glands that is mainly water with salts and other substances in it.

taste buds   Cells on the tongue that identify different tastes.

tissue   Groups of similar cells which form various body parts.

trachea   Windpipe.

valve   A flap of tissue that controls the flow of blood or other liquids in the body.

vein   Blood vessels that carry oxygen-poor blood to the heart.

vertebrae   Separate bones in the spine.

vibrate   To move back and forth.

viruses   Germs that grow in living cells.

vocal cords   Two strips of tough, elastic tissue and muscle stretched across the opening of the voice box in the throat that vibrate and produce sounds when air passes between them.

waste   The nonuseful solid parts of food that exit the body through the anus; called feces or stool.

Index

baby teeth, 94–95
backbone. *See* spine
blood:
    capillaries, 114, 119
    clotting of, 52, 54, 116, 119
    color of, 21, 114
    nutrients in, 116
    quantity of, 66–67
    veins, 114, 120
blood vessels:
    arteries, 117, 119
    broken, 52–55
    bruise, 55, 116, 119
    definition of, 114, 119
    dilation of, 115, 119
bones:
    hardness of, 44–46, 116
    joints, 48–50, 116, 119
    ligaments, 116, 119
    shape of, 47, 116
    vertebrae, 40–43, 115, 120
breath:
    moisture in, 78–81, 117
    volume of, 74–77, 117
breathing:
    exhale, 117, 119
    inhale, 117, 119
    model of, 70–73
bruise:
    definition of, 116, 119
    model of, 55

calcium phosphate:
    definition of, 116, 119
capillaries:
    definition of, 114, 119
    dilation of, 114
cells:
    definition of, 116, 119
    phagocytes, 116, 119
    platelets, 116, 119
    tissue, 116, 119
circulation:
    blood vessels, 52–55, 116, 119, 124
    bruise, 55, 116, 119
    capillaries, 114, 119
    clot, 52–54, 116, 119
    heart, 56–63
    scabs, 52–54, 120
    veins, 114, 120
clot:
    definition of, 116, 119
    scab, 52–54, 116, 120
cold:
    cause of, 117
    experiment, 82–85
    viruses, 117, 120
collagen:
    definition of, 119
cough, 82–85, 117
diaphragm:
    definition of, 117, 119
    model of, 72–73
digest:
    definition of, 117, 119

digestion:
    anus, 118, 119
    definition of, 117, 119
    digestive system, 96–103, 118, 119
    esophagus, 98, 99, 118
    experiments, 96–103
    peristalsis, 118, 119
    swallowing, 96–99
    teeth, 92–95
    waste, 118, 120
digestive system:
    definition of, 118, 119
    model of, 100–103
dilation:
    capillary, 114
    definition of, 115, 119
    eye, 106–109, 118
esophagus:
    definition of, 98, 118, 119
    description of, 98, 118
    model of, 99
evaporation:
    definition of, 115, 119
    skin cooled by, 22–24, 115
eye:
    camera red eye, 106–108
    model, 106–108
    pupil, 106–109, 118
feces. *See* waste
fingerprints:
    definition of, 8, 114, 119
    experiment, 6–9
fingertips:
    experiments, 6–9
    fingerprints, 8–9
    ridges, 6–8

friction:
    definition of, 114, 119
    experiment, 6–8
germs:
    definition of, 116, 119
    spreading of, 82–85
glands:
    definition of, 114, 115, 119
    sweat, 115
gravity:
    definition of, 116, 119
hair:
    curly, 30–33, 115
    cutting of, 34–36
    experiments, 26–38
    feeling in, 34–37, 115
    insulator, 26–28, 115, 119
heart:
    beats, 64–66
    shape of, 59
    size of, 56–58, 116
    sounds, 60–63
    squeezing of, 64–66
    stethoscope, 60–63, 116, 120
    valves, 116, 120
height:
    changes in, 42–43
insulator:
    definitions of, 115, 119
    experiments, 26–28
joint:
    definition of, 114, 119
    elbow, 48–50
    experiments, 48–50
    hinge joint, 48–50
    ligaments, 116
    thumb, 50

ligaments:
    definition of, 116, 119
light:
    colors of, 118
lungs:
    definition of, 72, 119
    exhale, 72, 117, 119
    experiments, 70–73
    inhale, 72, 117, 119
    model of, 72–73
    volume of, 74–77, 117
melanin:
    definition of, 114, 115, 119
    experiment, 18–20
milk teeth. *See* baby teeth
nerves:
    definition of, 116, 119
nutrients:
    definition of, 116, 119
oxygen:
    definition of, 116, 119
phagocytes:
    definition of, 116, 119
pigment:
    definition of, 114, 119
    experiments, 18–20
    melanin, 20, 114, 119
platelets:
    definition of, 116, 119
    experiments, 52–54
pupil:
    definition of, 108, 118, 119
    dilation of, 106–109
    model of, 96–108

respiration:
    breath, 78–81
    breathing models, 72–73
    cold, 82–85, 117
    cough, 82–85, 117
    diaphragm, 72–73, 117, 119
    exhale, 117, 119
    experiments, 70–73
    inhale, 117, 119
    lungs, 70–77, 119
    trachea, 117
saliva:
    definition of, 118
    digestion, 118
    tasting, 118
scab:
    definition of, 116, 120
    experiment, 52–54
sebum:
    definition of, 114, 120
senses:
    sight, 106–109
    taste, 110–113
    types of, 118
skeletal system:
    bones, 40-47, 115, 116, 119,
      120
    definition of, 115, 120
    spine, 40–43, 115, 120
    vertebrae, 115, 120
skin:
    color of, 18–21, 114–115
    dermis, 114, 119
    epidermis, 114, 119
    experiments, 6–24
    fingerprints, 6–9, 114, 119
    glands, 114, 115, 119

melanin, 114, 115, 119
nerves, 115, 119
oil, 14–16
pigment, 18–20
ridges on, 6–9
sebum, 114, 120
squames, 114, 120
sweat, 22–24
tanning of, 18–20
temperature of, 22–24, 115
waterproofing of, 14–17
wrinkles, 10–17
smell:
    experiments, 112–113
sneezing, 117
sound, 86–89, 117
spine:
    experiments, 40–43
    flexibility of, 40–42
    model of, 40–42
    spinal cord, 40–42, 115, 120
    vertebrae, 40–43, 115, 120
squames:
    definition of, 114, 120
stethoscope:
    definition of, 116, 120
    model of, 60–63
stomach:
    definition of, 118, 120
    experiments, 96–103
stool. *See* waste
swallowing:
    description of, 118
    experiments, 96–103
    model of, 99
    peristalsis, 118, 119

sweat:
    definition of, 115, 120
    experiments, 22–24
taste:
    experiments, 110–113
    smell's effect on, 112–113,
      118
    taste buds, 112, 118, 120
taste buds:
    definition of, 118, 120
teeth:
    biting, 92–94
    chewing, 92–94, 117, 118
    jobs of, 92–95
    milk teeth (baby), 94–95
    model of, 94–95
    shapes of, 92–95
    tearing, 95
tissue:
    definition of, 116, 120
trachea:
    definition of, 117, 120
veins:
    definition of, 114, 120
viruses:
    definition of, 117, 119
vocal cords:
    definition of, 117, 120
    model of, 86–88
waste:
    definition of, 118, 119
wrinkles, 10–17